Career Success

Preparing for your future

Jeff Davis

Copyright 2015 The Lordship Companies Inc. All rights reserved. No part of this book may be reproduced, stored in a retrieval system or transmitted by any means electronic, mechanical, photocopying, recording or otherwise, without the written permission from the author.

This book is dedicated to my wife Olivia who stuck by me when I had to recreate my career. Even when it looked like it would not ever work out she stuck with me. Today I live in the benefits of her faith in me and her commitment to being by my side, regardless.

"Treasure the wife of your youth for she is your greatest reward for all of your hard labors."
Ecclesiastes 9:9

Jeff Davis

The purpose of going to school and getting an education is to one day enter into a career that you enjoy. For that reason students and parents spend tens of thousands of dollars in the hopes that one day it will all pay off.

Sadly so many people go to school, study and graduate only to take a job for the wrong reasons. Instead of entering into a career doing what we love we just take a job. There are bills to be paid. And survival becomes the purpose of working.

Your future success is tied into your ability of finding something you love and making a career of it. When you love what you do motivation becomes easier to come by. It's not just a job; it is a lifestyle.

In this book you will see examples of concepts that when properly used will help you build a solid career.

Best wishes in your chosen profession!

Jeff Davis

Set Your Goals and Live Them

I believe the best way to hit your goals is to set them. Before you can ever achieve any real success you must first determine what that success will look like.

It is important that we strive each day to better ourselves. At least once a year we need to think about where the rest of our lives will be headed. Then we have to organize those annual goals into monthly, weekly, daily and hourly goals. It takes a lot of work to get things set up but once we do we will find that we can accomplish more in a year than we ever dreamed possible.

Let me share with you a few tips about goal setting. Now, there are tons of books on this subject so I am not going to be sharing any new revelations. But Since I have read many books on the subject I am compiling a few pointers to hopefully make goal setting a priority for you.

1) *Treat goals as you would your next vacation* - I live in California. If I plan to take a trip to Illinois I have to plan the following; when do I want to go (date), how do I want to travel (by air, plane, car), how long will I stay (days, weeks months) and what will I do when I get there. Goals do the same thing for us. If you have had a successful vacation you know you needed to plan it well. Goals are when we plan our lives well.

2) *Get the big plan in place* - Goals need to be large. I am going to travel from California to Illinois. That is not the same as walking to the corner store for a loaf of bread. Goals need to be similar to taking a long trip. If your goal is to make breakfast this morning it may not take a lot to get that done. But if you have a goal to make a lot of money, grow closer to your family or see some exotic cities in the world, it will take some goal setting.

3) *Obtain your goals by taking small steps daily*- break those goals down into weekly, monthly and daily activities. You need to keep your eye on the prize but in order to eat an elephant, it takes one bite at a time.

Set your goals! Live your life! Enjoy each day knowing you are getting closer to what you really want.

Gratitude Comes From the Right Attitude

The attitude you carry with you during your lifetime will greatly determine just how high you will soar. The more positive your attitude the more you will be able to accomplish.

There is one thing you can do to greatly impact your attitude and take it to new heights; that is to flood your mind and heart with gratitude.

When you look at your life and focus on all the things you have to grateful for, it's impossible to have a bad attitude because the good of your life will take over. You will be smiling at you consider all the good things in your life you have to be thankful for.

Here is an example of how gratitude can greatly impact your attitude. Try saying this as you consider the implications it has on how you look at your life;

"My eyes open us and I am excited because I have woke up to the fact that my life has so many good things in it today. I feel no pain. I can move my hands, legs and feet. I can look around and see the sun as it sneaks a peek into my room. I shake a little all over because today I feel good.

I walk to the bathroom and I look at a very handsome reflection in the mirror. I am grateful for the way I look, how I smile and what a life I have. I walk around and am so grateful to have a wife that loves me, children that I can parent and love back, a place to live in, clothing to wear, food in my refrigerator, a car in my driveway and places to go.

I leave home and feel the warmth of the sun on my face. It feels so good. I drive and pass by different people on the streets. I roll down my window and I smile at strangers. They think something is wrong with me but I know, there is so much right with me I can hardly contain myself.

I go about my work on a job that I love. I finish my day and head to a local restaurant to meet my wife and children for dinner. Tonight we are celebrating life. They think something is wrong with me. I am trying to tell everybody, I am so grateful. That is what is right with me.

I end my day saying goodnight to my children and a kiss to my wife. As I drift off to sleep I imagine how many people would love to have my life. Is it perfect? No. But am I grateful that this is my life and I get to live it?

Yes.

Whatcha Thinking

 Have you ever heard any of these statement; "whatsoever the mind can conceive and believe, it can achieve." How about "as a man thinks, so is he." Then there is "the man who thinks he can and the man who thinks he cannot are both right." Finally, "you can do it if you put your mind to it."

These and many other famous sayings come from the minds of men and women who have come to understand the power we all possess in our minds. The incredible ability to shape our future by harnessing the potential we carry within us.

We all begin our lives totally dependent on someone else to care for us. Babies cannot feed, clothe and provide for themselves. We need help. As children we receive as much help as is offered to us.

Just as we don't choose the person and vehicles they use to provide for us we also don't choose the mindset they carry with them. Some people have very healthy perspectives on life and view it as a place for winners to excel. They get up every day looking for their next opportunity to hit it big in this game we call life.

There are some who have unhealthy life perspectives. For whatever reason they have failed in some or all areas of their lives. They are negative, broken and very pessimistic in their outlook on life. Imagine what it is like to grow up in one of these two environments. Either you will find the possibility of success or the failure of defeat each day growing up.

People tend to voice what is in their hearts. A positive person says positive things. They look at life with the glass being half full. Negative people say negative things. They see the glass as half empty. Children hear and experience these words growing up. The effects are not only devastating but hard to change.

I was 5 years old in kindergarten. I was a good child but as all children, sometimes I got in trouble. I remember one day the principal called my mother to the school because the teacher said I was creating problems in the classroom. My mother was holding my hand and listening to the principal talk about how bad I was. I still remember the principal's words to my mother "your son has a habit of being outspoken. He is very opinionated and refuses to listen to what the teacher says. He is a failure at such a young age. You should seriously consider what you are going to do with him."

Instantly my mother turned and pointed her finger at me. I was preparing for a verbal thrashing. She said "don't you ever let anyone tell you that you are a failure. You can do and be whatever you want in this life. It's your choice." Then she turned and let the principal have it saying she would not tolerate anyone berating her child because he was still a child and needed guidance, not criticism. I went on 8 years later to graduate from that same school as valedictorian.

Allow your mind to dream. Be all you can be and be the best at it.

Winning is Possible

If you have chosen to embark on a career then you have chosen to take your life down a roller coaster ride. Life is full of the ups and downs; that is what makes life exciting!

Failure is inherent with the pursuit of a career. Most of the time you have to deal with people who don't like or need your skills. There is always an objection waiting for you to overcome. The financial pressure caused by you not producing results can be overwhelming. Add to this that most successful people are not happy when they fail and you have the perfect combination for wanting to quit.

Let me offer you some encouragement. Don't quit when you are working on your goal. You don't know if you will succeed with the very next blow. Stay on task, on course and watch what happens to the diligent.

IT WILL GET BETTER! Hard to believe but it's true. Things always look darkest before the dawn. There are times when it gets incredibly hard to go on and continue pushing. But we have to remember that life is in a constant state of flux and things always change. They go from bad to worse to better to good (not always in that order).

CHANGE IS GOOD! It may not look like it at the time, but change is a good thing. Consider how it was when man began to ride horses instead of walking everywhere. I know he must have felt relieved and a horse could travel farther and faster than he had done on foot. However in time we had the railroad train, automobile and airplane. These methods were all faster and carried man farther. People are always changing. So will you in your sales career. Don't neglect changes for they will help propel you to new heights.

QUITTERS NEVER WIN! Who remembers the guy who almost made it? The winner of the silver medal in the Olympics? The team who came in second best at the championship game? Although most of us forget their names the one thing we will remember is the person who quits. Coming in 2nd is very important because it means you tried your hardest to come in first. Not everyone will be a superstar but when you enter the game, stay in it no matter what.

WINNERS NEVER QUIT- Finally, in the words of Mr. Churchill, "never, ever, ever quit". Stay in the game. Keep going. In the end you will be a better person.

Success Happens on Purpose, Not by Accident

People look to make their lives happen in a big way. Most people do not want to spend life struggling trying to make ends meet. I believe people would much rather be a success than failure.

Success has its own definition depending on who is defining it. For some success means the freedom to do what you want to do. For others it means having all the financial resources you could ever hope for. Then there are those who put God or family at the top of their financial success list.

Whatever definition you choose to adhere to there are some principles that are non-negotiable. Such principles include:

UNDERSTANDING ITS HAPPENS ON PURPOSE - Success is not an accident. The people who start off on the journey to becoming successful rarely find it on accident. Typically it is the product of being extremely intentional.

Consider companies like Ford, Apple, Wal-Mart, Microsoft, Disney and Dell. Each leader of these companies had a dream, that dream motivated them to create something that looked like the fulfillment of their dream.

UNDERSTAND IT TAKES FOCUS TO BECOME SUCCESSFUL- Laser beams work because they concentrate light into a beam that can cut through steel. The power of a laser comes in being incredibly focused. When you study successful people they all have this uncanny ability to focus their attention on the task at hand. Although I know we live in the age of "multi- tasking" the real power comes from knowing how to stay focused until the goal is achieved.

Being the jack of all trades and master of none is not the secret to success. Instead focus your attention in one direction and refuse to quit until you see what you have been looking for.

UNDERSTAND IT'S POSSIBLE IF YOU REALLY WANT IT - All things are possible if you can believe it. Think about all the inventions we enjoy today (airplanes, computers, internet, long distance travel, etc.) and how they were in the imaginations of great men who thought about these inventions long before we saw them. In order for something to be, one must see.

Can you see yourself successful? Can you see yourself accomplishing your goals? Whatever you wish to achieve you must first believe and then conceive. Believe it is possible and conceive how it may come to pass. Then focus on doing what you need to in order to accomplish your goals.

Go get the success that is waiting for you to claim it!

Principles to Increase Your Success

We began in Success Principles 101 with the foundation for success. Principle 101 was "take 100% personal responsibility for your life". In this segment we will explore how to do that more effectively. We continue that thought with this article.

Our lives are the results of things that happen within us. Some of these things are good and others are bad. We don't always control the things that happen to us. But we can control the things that happen within us. We control how we will respond to the things (events, occurrences or whatever you want to call them).

With each thing/event we respond. This determines how things will turn out for us. For example, if you find a $100 bill on the ground walking home, you can go to the store and spend it all. You can spend $10 and save the rest. In one scenario you just spend till you would go broke. In the other you still spent (although much less) and ended up $90 richer.

What determines the end results? Was it the $100? Or was it the decision you made as to how you would use it.

Years ago I belonged to an Investment Club. We researched, purchased and sold stock as a group. I had a stockbroker who gave us advice on how to play the market. We had purchased some shares of a telecommunication stock. She told us to do our research and see if we wanted to increase our holdings. By her estimations the company was positioning itself to do something that would impact its stock price. We did our research and found they were looking to make some bold steps so we increased our holdings. The stock increased in price more than fourfold in a short period of time.

She told us if we were serious about investing in stock we had to watch the market and the companies we were invested in. You have to "know when to hold them and to fold them". Well we failed to look at the bigger picture. We were so excited about our new found wealth that we didn't keep watch on our stock. The company made some more moves that were not favorable in the market and the price plunged. We lost almost all of our profit from before. We sold at a small profit and the group became discouraged.

We made a decision based on an event in the marketplace and the result was an increase in our portfolio. Consequently we failed to respond to another event in the market and lost all that profit. Whose fault was it for our success? Our failure?

Taking 100% responsibility for your life means you own the outcome. Good or bad. We profited when we acted one way and lost when we acted another. It was our fault.

That's how life is. It is always our fault. Or so it would seem.

Success Principles

Do you compliment or do you complain?

That is a very simple yet pointed question. Life has many things that we can and should be grateful for. Family, friends, health, strength, life, money, career, mental awareness, etc., etc. When we look at all that we have to work with, do we compliment that through the words of our mouths.

"How is your family doing?" Do you say things like "great, wonderful."

"How do you feel?" Do you respond with "I feel good today."

When someone looks nice or smell nice, do you offer up a compliment? Do you let people around you know that you notice the things they do that are worth mentioning?

Or have you fallen into the habit of the complainer. Do you see the glass half empty instead of half full? Do you criticize the things you see wrong around you? Do you complain about what you don't have, can't do, won't accomplish or get to finish? Do you make excuses for failure and justify the reason you have not succeeded?

Successful people learn a critical element about success; you have to control your internal environment and work to have your external environment conducive to succeeding.

Internally, you have to do what I refer to as "self-talk'. I get up each morning and walk around my neighborhood and yes, I talk to myself. My neighbors have told my children "I see your father walking and talking each morning. Is he praying, or reading or both?" My daughter told them "He is probably doing both; my dad is known to talk to himself. But he is not crazy. He says it's the most intelligent conversation he will have all day."

You have to tell yourself you are successful. Not that you will be or that you hope to be but that you are. You have to internalize the whole concept of being a success right now. You have to see that everything you need to succeed has already been given to you. It's not money or education or family life that determines whether or not you will be successful; it's whether or not you can see that as you continue to live, you will get better and better, You will make a way for yourself that leads you to success.

In addition you must evaluate your external environment and eliminate those factors that contribute to failure. As a real estate investor I have had properties in low income areas. I believe all people need to have a place to live. But I don't believe all low income areas have to be dirty with trash all over the streets, insects living with people like tenants and folks not getting up till noon to start their day. I have said to tenants there "don't hate me because I like a clean block to come home to, a clean house to live in and I start my day early in the morning. There is a reason successful people succeed and failing people fail. The choice is yours. You have to decide the direction your life is going in. Then things in your environment will begin to agree with your expectations."

Compliment the things in your life that are good. Don't complain about the things in your life that are bad. Change what you can and get away from the things you can't. In time life can and will change for the better. You will love that it does.

Success Principles Again

Success leaves clues!

Success, like failure, is not an accident. It happens on purpose, whether we strive to do so or not.

There have been many books written about it, lectures and seminars given on it and yet even today many people are striving to find the key to lasting success.

What is success? It has different meanings to different people. Consider the following;

1) Family - for some having a happy, functional family with universal acceptance by all is success

2) Health - for some being healthy each day is a sign of success

3) Wealth - to others, you are not successful if you are broke

4) Prestige - being recognized as a leader in your field is success to many.

You have to determine your personal definition for success. What is success to some will not be the same to others. This definition will help you to identify what steps you need to take in order to reach the levels of success you hope for.

To begin this journey, I want to give you what I am calling Success Principle 101:

"You must take 100% personal responsibility for your life" Period! No exceptions, no excuses.

The tendency for many is to find blame for all the shortcomings in their lives. Yet nothing is further from the truth. In order to find lasting success, you must be responsible. You are not responsible for all that happens to you. But you are responsible for how you respond to all that happens to you.

Is the cup half full or half empty? Is the impossible possible or highly improbable? Can you make it or are you doomed to failure? Too many people blame their lot in life to someone else (I didn't have a father, my mother didn't love me, my siblings hated me, my boss held me back) or to something (I don't have a college education, I don't have the skills, I lack the experience, I am the wrong gender, wrong color and the list goes on).

And the list goes on.

True success will always allude us if we fail to realize that no one is to blame for how our lives turn out. You cannot impact what happens to you (sudden death of a loved one, unexpected illness, job loss, etc.) but you have 100% control over how you choose to respond to adversity. And it is your choice.

I want to encourage each and every one of you who wishes to have lasting success in life; Take responsibility for your actions.

Finding Success When You Fail

Failure is not optional. It is a part of living. There is no way to succeed in anything unless you can dealing with failing at some times. Failure is the prelude to great success. When you try to hit a home run, you have to be ready for a strikeout on occasion.

"Failure is not a single, cataclysmic event. You don't fail overnight; failure is a few errors in judgement, repeated every day - Jim Rohn."

"I do not believe in failure; it is not failure if you enjoy the process. - Oprah Winfrey."

We all make mistakes. And we have to take the time to learn from them. Otherwise it is a waste of time. Look at some of the legends we all appreciate and look up to. Michael Jordan missed thousands of shots in his career. In addition he has also lost close games and missed the gamed winning shot. Yet when you listen to him talk about failing he will give credit to winning because he failed.

I believe failing is contagious. When we find ourselves missing the mark often it is very easy to fall into the mindset that failing is normal. But nothing is further from the truth. With every adversity and failure we face there is an equal opportunity to find success.

Sports show us that no matter how great an athlete is, they will never hit a home run 100% of the time, shot the winning basket or score a touchdown. A great athlete will try even though they know they will not score all of the time. Babe Ruth was the home run king for years yet he also led the league in strikeouts. You cannot hit a home run unless you are willing to risk being struck out.

We have to do more in order to achieve more. We have to strive to gain greater heights than we ever had before if we want to be successful. It's like learning how to walk. Yes you will get knocked down. And you will fall often. But if you keep getting up, keep picking yourself up, you can and will eventually be walking.

I was on vacation with my family years ago and they were all in a 6 foot pool. They had learned how to swim and I was proud watching them. I got in the water (even though I could not swim) and slipped. I felt myself drowning in a 6 foot pool. Then it hit me; I am six feet tall so if I would just stand up and walk, eventually I would find my way out of that pool. You don't drown by falling into the water; you drown by staying there too long.

Make "NO" Your Best Friend

You will never survive in a competitive work environment if you cannot handle and deal with the word no. It is as common as word as any in our modern day language. It has been programmed into our minds from an early age and still lingers on in the mind of most.

Consider how we learned how to walk. Little children will climb over to a table, place their hands upon it and pull themselves into a standing position. They will look around for a few months, let go and take a few steps. Then they fall down. Do they quit? Do they tell themselves that failing to walk this time means they will not walk at all? Or do they crawl back to that table and try again? Children fall down lots of times before they finally get the hang of walking.

Consider what it took for them to get the courage to take that first step. Children start off on their backs getting love and attention for others. Then they learn how to roll over on their stomach. In that position they begin to learn how to crawl. At first they scoot along but in time they learn how to pull their legs under them, get on all 4 and crawl. This process can take weeks or even months to master. But these children are determined to get the hang of it.

Through continued efforts and hard work the child learns how to grab hold of things, stand up and walk, Now he is reaching for everything and the word he becomes very familiar with is "no". Don't touch this, stop it, I am going to spank you, he is so bad, etc. etc., etc. Negatives words create negative thoughts within him and without realizing it, the activity he once partook with unashamed resolve he must now stop it.

Most parents have no idea of how detrimental it is to associate the word "no" with activities that are positive. Learning to walk is positive. Exploring your environment is positive. Yes, there are dangers associated with children pulling things down on themselves or knocking things over. But the act of reaching for something higher is not bad; matter of fact, it is the very essence of success.

So reach for the stars. Try to accomplish more today than you did before. And resolve to never, ever give up, no matter how many "no's' you have to listen to.

Reach for the stars. You may hit the moon.

Guaranteed Career Success

There is wisdom in choosing a career path for your life. If you look at what you are good at and what interests you then you can choose a career that coincides with your gifts. Having a job can be a chore; having a career can change your destiny.

Why is this so? Many people go to work because they need to earn a living, take care of their responsibilities and pay their bills. But when you have a career that you really enjoy you would be willing to work for free (don't do that when you do have obligations to meet). People with a job that is in their lives only for their survival tend to want to be paid regardless.

If you are going to walk down the career path it helps to have a plan. You cannot leave something as important as your future success to chance. Below are some things you should consider when looking to solidify your career and enjoy some success;

1) Know your stuff - to be engaged in any career requires that you know what you are doing. Your career may be to own and run a landscaping company. You do not need to necessarily go to college to do this but you need to understand landscaping, sales, staff management and business oversight. Whatever direction you choose to go in it is best if you know your stuff.

2) Study your stuff - not only must you know your area of career choice you must become a student of it. This means taking time on a daily and weekly basis to become better at what you are doing. Many professions have continuing education classes, seminars and workshops that help you stay on the cutting edge of your career. Take advantage of these classes. Read about your career.

3) Commit to becoming an expert - if you study any discipline for 1 hour a day for the next 7 years you will know more about that subject than 90% of the population. It is not hard to become an expert when you focus on learning all you can about what interests you. Make this a priority.

Give your career the best that you have to offer. Be willing to become known as the best in your field. Give yourself an edge over your competition by being someone who is committed to building a career that matters.

Financial Success Can Impact Other Areas of Your Life

When you are involved in a career position it is easy to see the benefits financially. You will have more money, enjoy a nicer home, drive a nicer car, visit nicer places and save more money. Many people work strictly for the benefits that come from financial success.

Although these are definitely advantages to financial success, I think there are some benefits to having wealth that can make the rest of our lives very enjoyable. Let's explore how financial success brings success to other areas of your life;

1) *Freedom from worry* - people with money don't have to worry about the number one worry concern for most people, providing for their family. When you have adequate resources those worries tend to decrease and disappear altogether.

2) *Freedom from time* - money gives you the chance to do things that you typically cannot do when you don't have any. I remember owning my own business when I met my wife. I would stop by her job and see her at different times, drop by unannounced, etc. She would ask me how a man who was running a business had the time to do those things. I told her I had the money to pay people to work so I would be free to do other things with my time.

3) *Freedom to dream about your future* - would it not be nice to dream about going somewhere and knowing you can afford the trip before you start to dream? Financial success can give you the means to plan trips ahead of time, book flights and hotel rooms and visit places others dream about. It allows you to see the beauty in this wonderful world.

4) *Freedom to help others less fortunate* - finally it can allow you to help others who are less fortunate. When you pass a homeless person on the streets or you see a mother with small children struggling what do you do? I hope your heart goes out to them and makes you want to reach into your pocket and do something. When you have financial resources you can pick which option to utilize to help them out.

5) *Freedom to be yourself* - isn't it nice to be able to be who you feel you should be without having to worry about money? Whether your goal is traveling, artistic creation or just hanging out, money gives you the ability to do that and more.

Don't cheat yourself or your family of the benefits of financial success. Go get yours now.

This is Your Career

When it comes to your career you must be proactive. Even though we may go to school and get an education, it does not ensure career success. For those who have experience in their chosen profession you still have to work hard at it in order to find success.

A career is different from a job. In a job you work, get paid and provide for yourself and your family. You may hate what you do but endure it for the sake of a paycheck, A career is where you take your gifts, talents and abilities and plant them to watch your efforts grow and flourish. A career is well thought out and pursued with both determination and focus. You cannot develop a successful career without these two.

You will spend an average of 50 to 75 hours a week working in your career minimum given 168 hours each week that we all are given. There is the time we spend getting up to get ready to go to work, time traveling to work, doing our job, traveling home and removing our work clothes to relax and live our lives. Since this will take 30-45% of our total weekly time we should make sure it's time well spent.

Here are a few ideas for long term career success;

1) *Do something you enjoy* - it really hurts to have a job and not like what you do. Who wants to go to school to get an education to perform a job you hate? It is very important to work in a field you enjoy so that you can work with your heart content. Getting up and smiling on the way to work will do wonders for your self- esteem.

2) *Do something that matters* - we all need to feel that what we do matters to someone and counts for something. A job that means nothing to anyone will probably mean nothing to us. We all want to feel important and know that our career is necessary to someone.

3) *Do something that pays* - there are those who can work and not need to be compensated financially. For the majority of us that is not the case. Not only must we enjoy what we do and feel that it matters but it also must pay. Different professions have different levels of compensation. Strive to be compensated adequately for the work that you do.

Your Career Success is Up to You

Do you want a job or a career? When you have a job you get up and go to work, perform whatever duties are required of you and collect a paycheck. Many people who have jobs do so because they have to, not because they want to.

When you have a job that pays you enough to cover your bills it is very hard to quit it. Many times our jobs means we have a J.O.B. (just over broke) position and although we work 40 plus hours a week we never seem to get by. This makes us slaves to our positions and keep us from looking to have something better. A job can keep you trapped in a position that is very hard to get away from.

A career is something else. It starts with knowing what you want to do each and every day. You prepare for what you will be doing each day by getting a good education. Then once you enter the field you want to work in you actually go to work each day enjoying what you do. You don't have a job: you have a hobby that you love doing and getting paid for each day.

I know this situation first hand. I have had more jobs than any of my friends. I would take a position, stay a few months and then move on because the jobs became boring, I wasn't making enough money, etc. I believed that the answer was in finding the right "job". What I found is when you pursue a career in an industry you want to be in, you can create the opportunity that will allow you to flourish at your work space.

Let me offer a few suggestions about pursuing a career;

1) *Be true to yourself* - know who you are, what you want and why you want it.

2) *Do what you love, the money will follow* - don't chase dollar bills. Refuse to work strictly for pay. Instead tap into your passion. Find out what you are willing to do for free and let money be the side benefit.

People who have great careers tend to love what they do. When you are in that category you smile every day and become very grateful for the position you have.

I think finding what you love and then making it work for you is the best career choice anyone can make.

The Price of Success is everything

People look to be successful in life. The typical expectation.is that we can and will be successful because we are willing to try hard. We work from sun up to sundown and we will be successful in all that we do.

Although many wish that would be true, the fact is that it is not. The price one must be willing to pay is everything. But it's not always the "everything" people think it is.

I have had the pleasure of being both employee and employer. In this capacity you get to sit on one side of the interview desk trying to convince someone else that you are a good fit for their company. On the other hand as an employer you get to try to access whether someone will be a good fit for your company. Most times people focus on the resume and past performance to determine potential success. I know I have and sadly, it seldom works.

Let me begin with sharing with you four common fallacies that result from thinking success can come through only hard work;

1) Don't believe that future success is measured by what you have done before. Although the past is an indication of what you have been able to do, it is not the best indication of what you will do in the future. We must gauge our future success by our present performance. What you do today with the opportunity you have before you will determine how far you go.

2) Any time you have fallen into a slump take the time to learn more about the business you are in so that you can reinvent the way you approach it and make adjustments. Change is inevitable for future success.

3) Impatience due to working somewhere and not experiencing immediate success does not mean you are in the profession or career. It can mean you will need time to improve yourself to function at the level you believe you are capable of.

4) If you focus too much on your problems, you won't see your solutions. Every problem has a way to be fixed. The key is staying focused on your end result so that you can see what that solution is. Most of the inventions we use today came about because a problem existed and people worked diligently to find a solution that worked. In time they did just that.

The Best Job You Could Ask For

Once you are grown and on your own, undoubtedly you will need a job. The question is not whether or not you will find a job (given the state of our current economy it can be a challenge) but whether or not you will find the job you were created to do.

We spend on average 40 hours a week working. Take the time to get to ready for work, the time to travel to and from our jobs and you could easily spend 50 plus hours a week just doing work related events. There are 168 hours in a week so about 1/3 of our time is spent centering around this thing we call "work".

That being the case, we should try our best to have jobs that fulfill us. We need to be both challenged while performing our job and rewarded when we do a great at it. You cannot have these results if you go out and just "get a job". So many people go to work to earn a paycheck and provide for them and their families. This makes it hard to pursue the career that is meant for you if you are not fulfilled at your current position.

Am I saying quit your job? Not necessarily. What I am saying is you need to focus on what you want to do, what you love to do and what you would be willing to do even if you were not being paid. Focus the 1/3 of your life you spend working being as productive as possible while making the living you hope to have so you can enjoy life.

What is the best job you could hope for? I believe it is a job that offers you the following characteristics;

Financial Security - it is a sad thing to get up every day, spend all this time working and not earning enough to be secure. How much is that? Based on your budget you want a job that pays your bills, allows you to save a portion each paycheck and invest in your future. If I make $5000 a month and my monthly obligations are $3000 a month I have $2000 "margin" to work with each month. Margin is important in maintaining financial security.

Financial Freedom - this involves working to the point where you are not a slave to your job. It's been said that most people are only 30 days away from financial ruin. Can you take a month off, get no check from work and still live as you live with your job? If not, you are not free yet. Strive to get to the place where you have the reserves to hold you over even if you become unemployed.

Passive Income Sources - Let's say you have a good job and in addition you own real estate that gives you $2500 a month after the bills are paid. This is considered a passive income source. Increase these different sources for passive income and your job becomes much easier to work.

The best job to have is the one that allows you to grow into total freedom!

Are You the Best Worker Your Job Has Ever Seen

Are you the best worker your job has ever seen? Does your performance stand out from the rest of the crowd? If you are in management, do you lead the way? If you are not a manager are you one of the best employees your company has on payroll?

The tendency to excel is paramount if you want to experience success. Just getting by, being OK with mediocrity, having only what you need and no more is not the best way to move up the ranks to being seen as exceptional.

These are a few ideas about the way to become the best worker your job has ever seen:

1) *Get to work before your start time* - the early bird gets the worm. Get up early enough to make sure you get ready for the work you are about to do. It helps to spend a little quiet time by yourself, put your mind in the right framework and to hit the floor running.

2) *Have a game plan of action you can execute at work*- once you get to work you must be effective. This means having a plan you can execute. Wasting time is not an indication that you are a good worker. Most employees who are paid for 8 hours of work each day typically only work about 3 hours a day. The rest of the time is spent looking like they are working, focusing on personal projects and getting ready to go home.

3) *Cooperate with all co-workers*- the team focus is best for optimum results. If we can get everyone on the same page working towards one goal then our chances for great success increase exponentially.

4) *Do the best job possible for your company* - make sure your company looks good. Ensure they made the right decision by hiring you. Show why you are the best person for the job you have.

5) *If you are a leader at work, then lead by example* - people do best following a leader they can see before them. Sadly so many want to ascribe to the belief of "do what I say, not what I do." it is much easier to emulate successful behavior if you have an example you can put your hands on. Allow people to ask you questions about how you got to be such a good worker.

6) *Finally, be highly motivated* - nothing moves people more than motivation at a high level. Stay up. Get up so you can go up!

The High Price of Failure

Everyone seems to want to talk about success when it refers to making it big in life. I believe that most people would rather enjoy the benefits of being successful than the curse associated with failure.

Yet it is not possible to truly succeed without failure. That is hard for many people to believe but unless you know failure, you may mess up your future success. The reasons are many but a main one is to know that failure is the main way most of us learn success.

Here are some reasons failure cost us so much on the pathway to success;

1) *People who haven't failed yet tend to be over-confident* - It is amazing how cocky someone who has never tasted the sting of failure come across as the proverbial know it all. When you have never fallen it is easy to believe you never will. Yet for those who know failure falling is not a strange occurrence.

2) *Failure is never final*- many times after we fall down we feel like we can never get back up again. Yet the truly successful of our time have all failed at something in their lives. In order to be great you must take great chances on yourself. Many times we fall short. That does not mean we should never get back up again.

3) *Failure is what you have done, not who you are*- failure is an action. It is not final and it is not who we are. We are destined to do great things and in order to do that we need to see our actions as things we do but not who we are. You can do dumb things but that doesn't make you a dummy.

4) *Failure does not have to be fatal* - the worst mistake to make is the one that is fatal and cost you something you cannot get back. You drive your car and misjudge a curb so you go over the edge and hit the rocks. You failed to make the curb at a controllable speed and you died. That mistake won't allow you to go back and fix it. Some mistakes are one time mistakes. We can't afford to make them.

5) *Achievement is magnified after failure* - when you fail many times and then hit it big, it makes the success that much more memorable. Failure carries a high price but the reward of making it can be enormous.

Jeff Davis has seen his share of career challenges. He has followed his dreams only to see them dashed to the ground. Then to survive he took a "job" or two but could never get away from the feeling that his life was meant to more than he was experiencing. So with nothing but faith to go on he realigned himself and went after his dream.

Today he is President of The Lordship Companies Inc. a real estate investment company and insurance agency. He knows the value of pursuing what is in your heart.

He has written numerous books on the subject of finances, investing, real estate, sales, marriage and relationships.

He currently resides in Southern CA with his wife.

For information on his other resources visit Amazon and Createspace.

www.thelordshipcompanies.com

www.drjeffwrites.com

www.ingramcontent.com/pod-product-compliance
Lightning Source LLC
Chambersburg PA
CBHW072252200526
45168CB00015B/1694